T0380845

Print information available on the last page.

Rev. date: 07/01/2015

To order additional copies of this book, contact:
Xlibris
1-888-795-4274
www.Xlibris.com
Orders@Xlibris.com

THE LIFE AND JOURNEY OF
TRUCKSTOP
SHIRLEY

Inspired and Based on a True Story

Driven by P.R.I.D.E. Research

"For those who would learn the pathway to a successful journey"

P.R.I.D.E Must be the first thing
P.R.I.D.E Must be the second thing
P.R.I.D.E Must be the third thing

-Rev. Dr. Romando James, Ph.D.

Attribution Some rights reserved by kimberlykv

Rev. Dr. Romando James Ph.D.

For
Kyle and Keenan

My two sons who passed much too early

An
*Operation
Common Sense
With
P. R. I. D. E. Ministries*
Publication

What's the use of saying that you have faith and are Christians if you aren't proving it by helping others? Will that kind of faith save anyone?

James 2:14-The Living Bible

History of Anderson, SC

Anderson, South Carolina (SC) is located in the part of Anderson County, which sits in the Northwest corner of the state, on the banks of Lake Hartwell, which is a part of the Savannah River System that separates South Carolina and Georgia. Anderson was once the home and inhabited land of the Cherokee Indians. It wasn't until 1777 that the land, then called the Pendleton District, was given over to the Revolutionary War heroes Andrew Pickens and General Robert Anderson, by the negotiations of a treaty. The Pendleton district was split into two separate districts in 1826, named the Anderson and Pickens Districts.

Initially, the only courthouse in the districts was in Pendleton. This courthouse was at the top of the Anderson district nearest Pendleton, and because the other inhabitants of the county had a long way to travel, a second courthouse was built on the land that is now in the City of Anderson. Citizens of the district began to build houses around the new courthouse, thus creating a town by the name of Anderson Courthouse. Eventually, this town became know as Andersonville, and later, just Anderson. In 1833, the state recognized the city of Anderson in their legislature.

Anderson was known as a farming community for some time with much of its inhabitants being in the business of raising corn, cotton, or hogs.

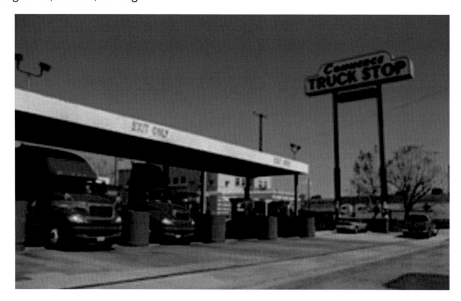

It was not until the 1800s that the textile industry began to boom in the area. William Whitner, an inventor from the area, was responsible for Anderson becoming the first city in the United States to have a continuous flow of electricity. The electricity was powered by a water mill in the area. Anderson County was first in the world to have an electrically-operated cotton gin. This is how Anderson received its nickname, "The Electric City."

Today, the Electric city is home to more than just electricity. Its economy is mainly manufacturing based. The city is located within 45 minutes of Greenville, SC, and within two hours of Atlanta, GA; connected by one of the Southeast's major interstates, Highway I-85.

Interstate 85 spans 668.75 miles from Virginia to Alabama. The major metropolitan areas through which it passes include Petersburg, VA, Charlotte, NC, Greenville, SC, and Atlanta, GA. The interstate became known as the I-85 corridor, bringing industrial and economic growth, and tourism. The truck transport traffic, which moves easily through the surrounding cities and towns, has been a great economic boost to the area since it was built.

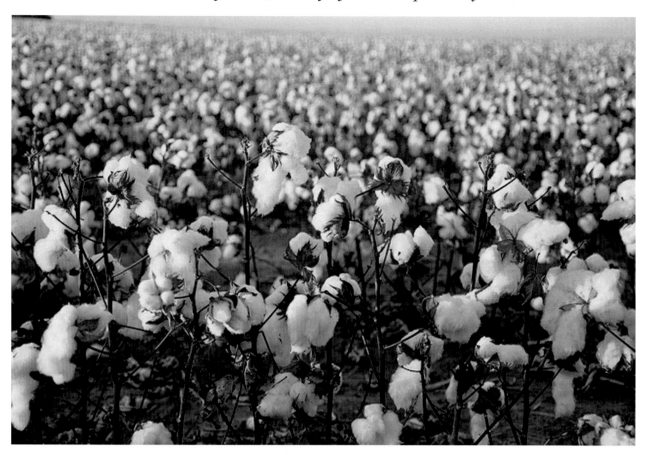

Introduction to P.R.I.D.E

"Whoever shuts their ears to the cry of the poor will also cry out and not be answered."
Proverbs 21:13

In this story you will meet a woman by the name of Shirley Estrich; a 6'5, 350 lb, size 15 shoe wearing woman who lives the journey of "rags to riches." I first met Shirley while passing through the truck stop where she worked. I was commuting between home and Atlanta, GA, where I was completing a second masters and Ph.D at Clark Atlanta University. Shirley possessed a tremendous life story and testimony, that I was inspired to share it with others.

Her life is more than just a story. For me, she is a hero. An African-American woman who has not only fought oppression, brutality, and prejudice in the south, but has been able to live and survive without bitterness or animosity towards those who wronged her. She models Christ in all of her ways and stands by the belief that *love's power overcomes hate's power*. Shirley also believes that there is a thin line between love and hate and she practices love because it is easier than practicing hate.

Shirley Shares Her Story

Shirley Estrich was born in Anderson County, SC, the eldest of 10 children born to her parents, L. T. and Clarina Mattress. Her siblings were: Margret, Clarence, Frank, Ruby, Willie C., Viola, Harrison, Frances, and Tina. In addition, four cousins lived with Shirley's family. All 16 members of the Mattress family lived in a small 3-bedroom house. The house was cramped and worn, but they made do with what they had to survive, as did many African Americans during that era. One night a rat came into the house through an opening in the floor and bit a toe off Shirley's left foot. Unsurprisingly, she has a rodent phobia to this day.

Her birth family were sharecroppers, growing cotton for the property owners. All family members worked, starting as young children. Shirley often picked over 300 pounds of cotton daily, far more than anyone else in the family, including the men. If the family did not meet their daily quota, they would be punished, children included. When Shirley was older, she married Charles Lewis Estrich and they had four children: Aaron, Sandra, Christopher and Sonjie.

Now 80 years old, she recalls how in the days before segregation, several white men sat at a table of the truck stop where she worked. They were very upset when she came to wait on them as a server for the stop. At first she did not know how to handle them and she remembers something from her days in the cotton field: just show love and a smile, but also look them dead in the eye and don't blink, just smile. From that point on she had no problems with them.

Mrs. Estrich became the first black woman in South Carolina to manage a truck stop. She learned from her bosses at the truck stop, Mr. and Mrs. Hendrix, how to wait tables, sit up straight, and to never be intimidated by race or class. This woman's life is an example of how some white families and black families existed together during the days of Jim Crow.

Shirley's Role in developing Cherokee Run Truckstop on Highway 1-85

Shirley worked as a sharecropper till she was 19 years old. After a severe boll weevil attack devastated the cotton harvest, the owners of the land sold the property. With no more work to do on the property, the owners, Mr. and Mrs. Pruitt, took Shirley to the Sandra Ann Truck Stop on U.S. Highway 29 South, owned by Mr. and Mrs. Hendrix.

It was at the Sandra Ann Truck Stop that she began learning the basics of maintaining a full service rest stop for truckers. However, the Sandra Ann stop lost business when the I-85 route became the preferred travel route for truckers. Mr. and Mrs. Hendrix, being savvy business owners, closed down their Sandra Ann stop to build a stop off Cherokee Run.

When the Sandra Ann stop closed, the only job that was available for Shirley during the building process of the Cherokee Run stop was driving a bulldozer. When asked if she would be willing to drive a bulldozer, her response was, "If I'm taught, I can do it just as well as a man." Shirley was offered two weeks of training in driving bulldozers. She began the third week driving the bulldozer and did better than most men. Not only did she operate the bulldozer, but she was also involved in the construction of the truck stop, where she was a cook and waitress, and eventually the manager.

The significance of her role and impact on 1-85 can be viewed in the article published Sunday, September 7, 2014, in the Anderson Independent, titled *111-85 has driven Anderson growth for 50 years*. Although she is not mentioned in this article, she was there during this time of development, for 30 years.

Saturday, November 1, 2014 — WEEKEND — The Journal **B1**

Shirley hits the stage

'Truckstop Shirley' opens tonight at CLT

BY GREG OLIVER
THE JOURNAL

PENDLETON — Shirley Estrich has inspired many since the former truck-stop worker's story made the print and electronic media a number of years ago. Now, her story is hitting the stage in three live performances this weekend at Clemson Little Theatre.

Two performances will take place today, at 3 p.m. and 7 p.m. There will also be a Sunday matinee at 3 p.m.

"We're expecting individuals from all over the state, as well as out of state — including former students and research assistants — to be in attendance as a show of support," said Romando James, the writer, producer and director of the play. "We're expecting a great crowd."

James said Estrich herself will be in the drama that begins in the cotton fields where she grew up working on a sharecropper's farm in rural South Carolina. The sharecropper's wife encourages her to take a job at a truck stop less than two miles up the road from the farm. She does just that and eventually earns the name "Truckstop Shirley."

The Clemson University professor emeritus said the scenes will depict her vivacious approach toward life, even in the face of great prejudice. He said Estrich dispenses wisdom and an infectious laugh that truck drivers, customers and co-workers learned to love and appreciate.

James first met Estrich at an interstate truck stop near Fair Play in the mid-1980s. The two soon struck up a conversation, and James told Estrich he wanted to make her the subject of his doctoral dissertation. Estrich, in turn, encouraged James to not give up on his doctoral pursuit, adding, "You never let a dream die."

After their initial meeting, James said he went to work developing Estrich's experience as one of six documentaries based on his "Common Sense with P.R.I.D.E. (Purpose, Respect, Integrity, Determination and Discipline and Enthusiasm)"

research. His efforts were expanded into a film documentary and a stage production, and now a possible movie is in the works.

This evening's performance will be recorded and sent to various studios and producers, including Oprah Winfrey, Steve Harvey and Tyler Perry, in the hopes of an eventual movie version.

During the summer, Estrich visited the Littlejohn Community Center in Clemson and told The Journal she never allowed the prejudice she encountered to affect her.

"You're not going to defeat me — I give you respect and you give me respect," she said.

A five-piece band and local choir will accompany the performances, and various school and church groups are expected to be in attendance this weekend. One

of the groups is the Wilderness Way Girls Camp in Fair Play

"Shirley got her start in Fair Play, and they read these articles about how she is plain spoken and down to earth," James said. "She came up similar to the way a lot of these girls did. She was beaten, she was bruised, she was rejected — but she rose up to be a manager.

She wants them to understand they can make contributions to society in spite of who they are and where they are now."

James said the Wilderness Way Girls Camp will be recognized at Sunday's performance and that he and Estrich will go to the camp and talk to the girls about P.R.I.D.E. during Black History Month in February.

Camp director John Bowman said he was intrigued after

PHOTOS SPECIAL TO THE JOURNAL

Shirley Estrich, pictured here with Clemson African-American Museum president Robert Kemp, has grabbed the attention of the media in recent years with her story of perseverance.

Shirley Estrich, the inspiration behind "Truckstop Shirley," will participate in a play about her life taking place this weekend at Clemson Little Theatre. Tapes of the production will be sent to various producers in hopes of making a movie version.

learning about Estrich from previous articles written about her in The Journal.

"She seemed like a neat person for the girls to get to know, about how she was able to handle adversity, working with people who don't always agree with you," Bowman said. "Her personality and character was such that we showed the girls the article and that she would be a neat person to meet."

James said he has received invitations to present "Truckstop Shirley" throughout the state, including Spartanburg, Columbia, Orangeburg and even as far as Tampa, Fla. Sequels to "Truckstop Shirley" are also planned in the next several years, including "Shirley Gets Her GED," "Shirley Visits New York City" and "Shirley Enrolls at a University."

A book, titled "The Life and Journey of Truckstop Shirley," is also in the works.

Kianna Gilchrist, who is in charge of tickets and photography for the "Truckstop Shirley" performances this weekend, said she is excited to be part of bringing the life of Estrich to the stage. She said meeting Estrich in person was an experience to be treasured.

"She's not a shy person and is very good about giving advice," Gilchrist said. "She's like a really grounded person in her faith and has a lot of life experiences."

'She was beaten, she was bruised, she was rejected — but she rose up.'

Romando James

Tickets for the shows, which are $15 for adults, $7 for college students with ID and $5 for those under 19 years old, can be purchased at the door. Proceeds from the two-act performance will benefit Clemson African-American Museum, Littlejohn Community Center and Crying in The Wilderness Prison Ministry.

A reception will be open to the public at 9 tonight at the University Inn, formerly known as the Ramada Inn, on U.S. Highway 123/76. During that time, the public will have an opportunity to meet Estrich and others affiliated with the performance.

Receptions will take place at 5 p.m. today and Sunday at the Clemson Little Theatre and are open to the public. For more information about the receptions as well as the play itself, call James at (864) 650-2891.

goliver@upstatetoday.com | (864) 973-6687
Follow on Twitter @JournalGO

LOCAL

I-85 has driven Anderson growth for 50 years

By Abe Hardesty
abe.hardesty@independentmail.com
864-260-1252

When Interstate 85's four lanes quietly opened on Sept. 8, 1964, South Carolina's first interstate highway drew little fanfare.

Miles from downtown Anderson, the road opened without ribbon-cutting, political speeches or extensive news coverage. It was described as "a supermodern, controlled-access highway" that would someday spread to 668 miles in length. But when highway patrolmen removed the barricades at 8 a.m. that Tuesday, Anderson residents were more concerned about Hurricane Dora.

Spinning near the Florida coast, the storm threatened to follow the path of Hurricane Cleo, which just a month earlier had dumped 3.15 inches of rain on Anderson in one day — part of a record-high 77.4 inches that soaked the city that year.

Fifty years later, Dora and Cleo are long forgotten. But I-85 continues to mold the future of Anderson.

Anderson was the focus on the last segment in South Carolina's 106-mile part of I-85 in the summer of 1964, when a 13-mile stretch from Liberty Highway (now Exit 21) was linked to the intersection of U.S. 29 (now Exit 34).

That ignited commercial development, boosted land values, made new work for road construction crews and sparked new interest from national chain stores.

Less than a year after the arrival of I-85, two primary links to the road — Clemson Highway and Old Greenville Highway — were transformed into four-lane roads from downtown Anderson. Within 10 years after its completion, real estate near I-85 doubled in price throughout the Upstate.

Built at a cost of $267 million, the South Carolina section of I-85 transformed the Upstate economically. In 1993, Business Week referred to "The Boom Belt" as a 30-year success story along I-85 that provided lessons for the rest of the country." Three years later, The Wall Street Journal pointed to the same corridor as a magnet for manufacturing.

Today, economic geographers such as T. Bruce Yandle refer to the region as "Charlanta," a 250-mile Mayfield-turned-commercial ellipse that powers the nation's third-largest economic region. Only the more established corridors of Boston-to-Washington, and the Chicago area, are busier economic belts today.

"I-85 defines the region,"

Cars and trucks fill lanes near exit 39 of Interstate 85, a freeway that has grown in 50 years to be a vital route in South Carolina and beyond.
NATHAN GRAY/INDEPENDENT MAIL

A car is driven north on S.C. 178 in Anderson, past signs for I-85.
KEN RUINARD/INDEPENDENT MAIL

Cars are driven on I-85 in Anderson County as rains fill the road before July 4 this year.
KEN RUINARD/INDEPENDENT MAIL

Trucks, a big part of I-85 traffic, zoom by near mile marker 18.
NATHAN GRAY/INDEPENDENT MAIL

said Yandle, dean emeritus of Clemson University's College of Business & Behavioral Science. "If that route had gone somewhere else ... that area, instead of this one, would have been the economic path."

The I-85 route, which includes 10 exits in Anderson County, follows the Atlanta-to-Charlotte railroad line built 82 years earlier. Two other routes were considered, one slightly to the west, following U.S. 123, and one further east near Greenwood.

Anderson's 37-mile slice is the state's largest of the 106-mile I-85 pie.

Just as that railroad line brought western South Carolina from what Yandle calls "the backwaters of economic activity" in the 19th century, I-85 became a conduit for 20th century growth.

"It is because of the I-85 belt that the Upstate is a dominant economic region in South Carolina," Yandle said, "and the reason the Upstate compares well to the rest of the state in terms of income, education, well-being and educational standards."

The impact of the highway quickly became apparent, as dozens of national retail chain stores took a new interest in Clemson Highway, which soon became known as Clemson Boulevard. In 1973, Michelin broke ground on a

commercial manufacturing plant, a 1.4-million square foot facility just three miles from I-85's Exit 19.

"We're living in a world where inventory is no longer sitting in local storefronts. The inventory is located in those trucks moving up and down the interstate," Yandle said. "Those trucks are mobile warehouses, and it's critically important to the growth of any city to be near them."

The road inspired entrepreneurs like Frances Crowder to build an international business without leaving town. I-85 gave customers in 25 states and three Canadian provinces easy access to his computer software firm in downtown Greenville.

"They could fly into Greenville and in just a few minutes be in my office, and yet I could do that while living in Anderson," said Crowder, now retired from business and an Anderson County Council member.

Today, the same road connects his beloved Anderson countryside with entertainment venues.

"We can enjoy something at the Peace Center and in a short drive come back home to Anderson County, where there's not wall-to-wall traffic," Crowder said.

Too young to drive when I-85 opened, Anderson native and Mayor Terence Roberts is often reminded often of its present impact.

"In terms of job growth and quality of life, there's no question that I-85 has helped us," Roberts said. "One example is Skins' restaurant, which started with one store in Anderson and now is a regional restaurant of 12 stores. They probably couldn't have done that without the interstate."

Matt Thrasher, part of the management team at Skins' Hot Dogs, said Clemson Boulevard was the first expansion target when it added a store in 1989.

"Everything seemed to be

INSIDE

Read about area residents' memories and see a timeline of I-85 construction. **7C**

ONLINE

To see photos of Interstate 85 over the years, visit **www.independentmail.com**.

moving in the direction of Clemson Boulevard. All the major retailers were moving to the mall and surrounding areas," Thrasher said. "We felt we have to have a store on that side of town to take advantage of the traffic."

Thrasher said I-85 "opened up Greenville and Georgia to us."

The interstate altered the residential landscape, creating housing booms near S.C. 81 and S.C. 153 that have since resulted in construction of at least five new schools in those areas.

As the city continues its slow stretch toward I-85, there are commercial casualties. Less traffic in the eastern part of town leads to less growth and fewer jobs.

"Urban growth and population studies tell us that things always grow toward the interstate," Roberts said. "That's apparent when you look at Anderson, Greenville and Spartanburg."

In a 30-mile stretch from the north end of the county to Main Street, a driver today would find only a handful of restaurants, none of them national chains, and a few past-their-prime motels. That's a dramatic contrast to the 1950s, when U.S. 29, carried heavy traffic through Anderson on its way from Baltimore to Pensacola, Fla.

City planners often ask Yandle how to avert decline and stagnation on the non-interstate side of town.

"There's no way to avoid that," Yandle said. "Retail stories want to be near a high-traffic artery, so an interstate pulls everything in its direction. Everything else becomes less cost-effective."

In some situations, Yandle has observed what he calls "equalization," which occurs when the cost of land and congestion near the interstate inflates to a point where investors buy elsewhere, he said.

He doesn't foresee that in Anderson soon.

"Not in the case of I-85," Yandle said, "because it has continued to grow. By widening I-85 a few years ago (in 2003), I-85 kept its advantage.

"The Charlanta belt is big. The force is with us, and I think it's going to continue to be an advantage for a long time."

Follow Abe Hardesty
on Twitter @abe_hardesty

A Model for P.R.I.D.E

Shirley's story became my story because she was the perfect model for my P.R.I.D.E. paradigm. Operation P.R.I.D.E was created with a mission and vision to lead and encourage youth, especially inmates, into a personal and growing relationship with common sense and pride by encouraging them to maximize and pursue the following creed:

P---PURPOSE: Develop a purpose that is positive to which you are fully committed.

R---RESPECT: Practice and learn to respect yourself, as well as others, regardless of race, background, religion, or spirituality.

I---INTEGRITY: Practice truth, honesty, and loyalty to your purpose regardless of the cost.

D---DETERMINATION and DISCIPLINE: These two qualities must never cease as you develop and solidify your purpose

E---ENTHUSIASM (Enthuse): To be proactive and to integrate the above rites of passage to ensure and bring solidarity to your spirit of God-given purpose.

These five characteristics are aimed to create a continuous cycle of achievement in future success. These characteristics will assist in developing life skills ranging from effective decision-making to leadership and business management. Although this will be a slow and steady process that will take time and patience with yourself and others, you must be willing to put in the effort to receive the reward. We're reminded of the need to practice patience in Aesop's Fable.

Aesop is the story of a poor farmer who one day visits the nest of his goose and finds at her side a glittering golden egg. The farmer then decides to take it home, where he learns, to his joy, that the egg is actually pure gold. Every morning thereafter the farmer gathers one golden egg from the nest of the goose and soon becomes very wealthy.

As the farmer grows rich, greediness and impatience turn into unfounded frustration when he becomes unsatisfied with the output of the goose and her golden eggs. In an attempt to get all the gold at once, he kills the goose and opens her up to find nothing.

The moral of this fable reflects how we, like the foolish farmer, often emphasize short-term results at the expense of long-term prosperity. Indeed, it seems that we are often more concerned about doing things speedy and efficiently, instead of doing it right and patiently. In his attempt to be efficient and quick the farmer became grossly ineffective; he destroyed his access to long-term results that provided a secure life.

As you read this story, while implementing P.R.I.D.E, try not to speed this process along, like the farmer. Commit to each and every aspect of growth with patience and reflection to live a life like Truckstop Shirley has.

The P.R.I.D.E Approach

Operation P.R.I.D.E is a project based in Clemson, SC, that is designed to help youth and adults, especially incarcerated individuals, use positive African rituals to move into adulthood and beyond. The acronym of P.R.I.D.E represents the concept of purpose, respect, integrity, discipline, and enthusiasm. The rituals associated with the rites of passage are important in the P.R.I.D.E approach that helps to highlight key moments in the rhythm of the individual's life when the values of society are transferred.

There are many examples in traditional African societies where rites of passage are used. In Igboland (West Africa), young people receive instructions in the values of the community. Some of the values transferred include self-esteem, respect for elders, perseverance, purpose, rectitude, ambition, self-control, and bravery. In Kenya, initiation rites have great educational purpose that mark the beginning of acquiring knowledge such as respect for elders, perseverance, purpose, obedience, bravery, hard work, and respect for one another.

P.R.I.D.E relationship to Kwanzaa

Some aspects of the P.R.I.D.E rites of passage are elements from Kwanzaa. This unique African American celebration focuses on the traditional African values of family, community responsibilities, commerce, and self-improvement. Kwanzaa means, "first fruit of the harvest", in the African language Kiswahili and is based on these Nguzo Saba (seven guided principles).

1. **Umoja-** Unity stresses the importance of togetherness for the family and community.

2. **Kujichagulia-** Self-determination requires that we define our common interest and make decisions that are in the best interest of family and in the community.

3. **Ujima-** Collective work and responsibility remind us of our obligation to our past, present, and future, and that we have a role to play in our community, society, and the world.

4. **Ujamaa-** Cooperative economics emphasizes our collective economic strength and encourages us to meet common needs through mutual support.

5. **Nia-** Purpose encourages us to look within ourselves and to set personal goals that are beneficial to the community.

6. **Kuumba-** Creativity makes use of creative energies to build and maintain a strong and vibrant community.

7. **Imani -** Faith focuses on honoring the best of our traditions. It draws upon the best in ourselves and helps us strive for a higher level of life for human-kind by affirming our self-worth and confidence in our ability to succeed and triumph in righteous struggling.

How Shirley's P.R.I.D.E. Captured
and Challenged Life Lessons

Shirley's success, survival and life-skills demonstrated that she has captured the P.R.I.D.E model as well as the Kwanza model in that she demonstrated her P.R.I.D.E. through her counseling from the cotton field to the truck stop.

P---PURPOSE: Shirley's purpose demonstrated that the power of love is stronger than the power of hate by showing her family and community that a sharecropper could go on to own the land she worked upon to on down a path of success to become a manager of a major truck stop on Highway 1-85 in South Carolina.

R----RESPECT: Shirley demonstrated respect for herself and others regardless of race, religion or background. It didn't matter how much cotton they picked, nor their size of the trucks or buses they drove.

I-----INTEGRITY: Shirley's integrity, demonstrated through unwavering truthfulness and honesty, was above approach in all of her ventures.

D-----DETERMINATION and **DISCIPLINE:** These two roots enabled Shirley to prove that a black woman could survive in any environment, no matter how hostile.

E------ENTHUSIASM (ENTHUSE): Shirley's strong faith in God helped her though every challenge she faced. This faith, which served as Shirley's roots, controlled the fruits of all her actions.

Shirley connected her purpose, respect, integrity, determination, discipline, and enthusiasm to the spirit of God.

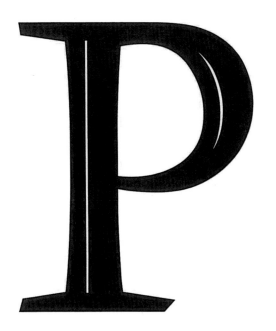

CHAPTER 1:

PURPOSE

Shirley Mattress Estrich lived on Route 9, Lee Dobbins road in Anderson, SC. For three generations the Mattress family lived on the land owned by Mr. and Mrs. Pruitt. Shirley and her large family were sharecroppers for twenty years. From the age when she could walk and pick cotton, Shirley's life was centered on supporting and helping every member of her family. When she would eventually work apart from her family at the truck stop, she held onto the value of knowing how purpose plays a role in working with and supporting others.

There are very few things that will cause Shirley to pause when she assist's another individual. Shirley's a competent woman who can do a lot by herself, but if a rat is around, Shirley will go the other direction. One night at age 9, while she was asleep a rat bit her toe, nearly to the point of tearing it off. Rats and other rodents came in and out of her house like they paid rent. She did not realize the amount of damage to her toe until she grew up to be a pretty sized girl with a 6'1, 225 pound stature.

One day she said to her mother, "Mother, why is my toe shaped weird?" Her mother replied "It's because a rat bit you on the toe when you were asleep." She never once woke while her mother stitched her toe up with an old time remedy of spider webs and turpentine. Ever since then, Shirley has had a great fear of rats. In her house today, you will find her feeding rats only poison, to kill them within 24 hours.

The tenant farmhouse where her family lived was about a half mile across the road and was surrounded by stray cats. One day a cat bit her on her right leg. Shirley, being unafraid of cats, took the cat and threw it out the back door so hard it was the first time that anyone had seen a cat die from being thrown.

On another occasion, Shirley and her family were in the yard playing hopscotch when a stray dog came running down barking angrily. Her mother told her and her sisters and brothers to run from the dog, so they ran and tried to get back to the house. Shirley, coming to the defense of her family, picked up the dog and threw it across the field. The dog died in the same way as the cat.

Shirley's mother became sick during Shirley's youth and was not always able to keep up with all ten children. This resulted in Shirley taking care of all her brothers and sisters, which forced her to prioritize family over school. Shirley spent most of her time at home taking care of her sick mother, during the time her baby sister Tina was born. It was important that her younger brothers and sisters stayed in school. She dropped out of school officially in the 11th grade, the same year that her mother passed away. She feels the experience of taking care of her brothers and sisters is what triggered her P.R.I.D.E.

Shirley picked cotton for her family from sun up to sun down, picking 300 pounds of cotton daily for nearly 20 years . Around 18 years old she began to experience an urgency to develop a purpose in life that didn't involve picking cotton. However, she never lost sight of the value of working side by side with her family to survive and thrive.

At some point in time, Shirley asked her father if she could get a job, and he told her to wait until she was nineteen years old. When she turned nineteen, she got pregnant and had a little boy, forcing her father to allow her to get a job.

Shortly thereafter, the landowners took her to a truck stop, where she started washing dishes under the Hendrix's, who owned the truck stop. While washing dishes, she would also help in food preparation. The stop only had two tables in the station where blacks could eat and drink coffee. There were many more tables for the white patrons. The white drivers had a place to sleep on beds; the black drivers slept on rugs on the floor.

During her shifts at the stop she counseled the blacks as well as the whites on what to eat, what not to eat, drinking while driving, picking up prostitutes, relationships, and family matters. Truckers came from all over the place to see her. She earned the nickname of big mama and big foot. It was in that truck stop her life's purpose was reaffirmed. Since childhood and even now, Shirley was meant to guide and help people along their life routes regardless of racial identity.

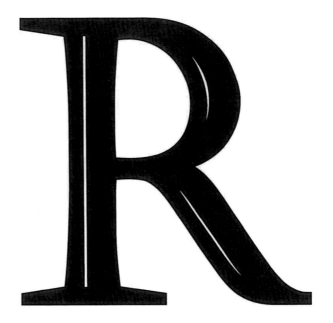

CHAPTER 2:

RESPECT

Shirley developed her respect under the condition of being a sharecropper because she recognized that many of her family members could not meet the quota of picking 300 pounds of cotton per day, including her mom and dad. Her love for her family and landowners motivated her to pick 300 pounds of cotton to make up the difference for those that could not.

Respect for self and others is often a forgotten and seldom practiced value, but it is one Shirley keeps at the forefront of her mind. Truckstop Shirley was introduced to that value of respect at an early age. She was in the first grade when she began to recognize that she was bigger and stronger than anyone in her class. Because of this size, she thought she did not have to have respect for anyone, especially boys.

One Tuesday afternoon, during recess, she began to bully the smallest boy in her class. She tried to force him off the swing set and when he refused, she pulled him in an attempt to take his seat. This event became the first challenge that she had ever faced because "Lil Mike" decided to stand up against the big bully. He, with one push, knocked Shirley on her rear end, and got on top of her, beating her until she cried. The teacher, Mrs. Johnson, was the only one who saved her. To this day, Shirley has never forgotten her lesson of being a bully. Lil Mike taught her how to respect the rights of others.

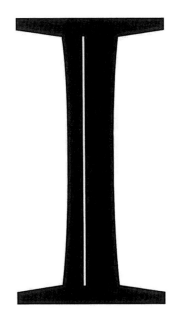

CHAPTER 3:

INTEGRITY

Shirley's value for working with people was grounded in honesty and truthfulness that never wavered. Her *yes's* were *her yes's* and her no's were her no's. In her time, Shirley Estrich has done everything from pick cotton and bounce drunks, to cook up a meatloaf so sweet it might tempt angels down from heaven just for a taste. I gave her the name "Truckstop Shirley" because I discovered that truckers from the north, south, east, and west would often stop by just to taste some of mama's cooking and receive wise counseling.

As a doctoral student in Counseling and Psychology, I was assigned to find a community person with a story that would support my Ph.D. paradigm for Operation P.R.I.D.E. While interviewing Shirley, I discovered that her integrity was grounded years before her truck stop experiences. She recounted a story that happened to her in eighth grade that illustrated her integrity well.

Shirley always thought she could never do math. For this reason, she copied off of the classwork of Grace Mary Hall. She always positioned herself in the classroom so that she could copy off of Grace's paper. One day, Grace decided that she was fed up with Shirley copying off her paper, so during the final exam, Grace purposely wrote down the wrong answers because she knew that Shirley would copy them. After Shirley finished copying, she turned in her test, only to find out that Mary Grace changed her answers back to the correct ones. Shirley failed the exam, and from that moment on, she learned to rely on herself to study and learn the material on her own. Her integrity not only progressed in Math, but in other subjects as well. This lesson prepared her for a life journey guided by honesty and truthfulness.

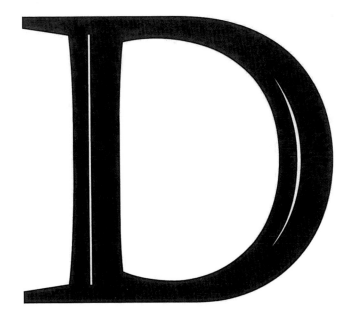

CHAPTER 4:

DETERMINATION & DISCIPLINE

"Everything starts out with a seed of desire" (The Winning Mind, Craig Lock). This desire comes from a person's want to succeed and accomplish their life goals. The path to achievement comes with many obstacles and hardships. Determination gives you the resolve to continue working despite challenges along the way. One must possess self-discipline in order to succeed. Shirley embodied both of these roots for her to succeed in counseling her fellow cotton pickers, land owners, family members, and truck drivers. It did not matter to Shirley who they were. She practiced and passed on determination and discipline to everyone she encountered. One example stands out.

A truck driver from Miami stopped at the truck stop and asked Shirley for advice about his weakness for picking up female hitchhikers despite being married. He could not control the desire to break his marriage vows as well as his vows to God. After counseling with Shirley, she instructed him on how to manage his determination and discipline by repeating in his mind "Never, never, never, never, never will I put my wife, my children, my life, my body, and my commitment to God in a compromising position." This Miami driver called Shirley one year later and told her that her advice had worked. Now, several years later, he is still in touch with Shirley and he continues to use determination and discipline as a foundation to be true to his wife, family, and God.

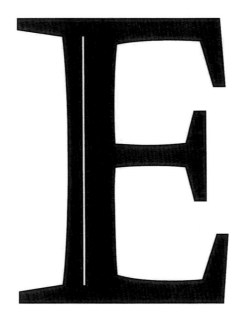

CHAPTER 5:

ENTHUSIASM

Desire gives birth to the various passions in life. Passion directs your purpose and drive in each action. Without passion, your life has no meaning and direction, everything that you do will be void of zeal and enthusiasm. Shirley is not passive about her passion, which is grounded in the Spirit of God. She never passes an opportunity that will allow her to encourage any and every one that she meets with a high degree of energy and enthusiasm; leading with her trademark, a big wide white smile. This was noted by news anchor Michael Cogdill from WYFF4 News of Greenville, SC many years ago. This infectious smile seemed to uplift truck drivers' spirits despite their problems. Also, she encouraged women on special trips that would often come into the truck stop for coffee and rest. She encouraged inmates in prison, school children, and families with problems. Shirley gives credit for her effective counseling to her enthusiasm and smile because she is not passive about her passion to please God first, and her fellow man second.

A white man named Fred came into the diner one day with his friends. He did not want a black person to serve him. Shirley met him with love and enthusiasm and explained that black people operated the establishment and provided the same quality of service as that of a business ran by anyone else. Her enthusiasm changed Fred's view as he became a regular customer with no qualms as to who served him. He even began to bring Shirley birthday gifts each year to show appreciation.

Shirley believes there must be a zero tolerance for any behaviors that damage anyone whether it is towards racial, physical, or mental differences. Shirley can often be heard stating that her enthusiasm and strength come from John 15:4, 11Remain in me and I will remain in you." No branch can bear fruit by itself. It must remain on the vine. Truckstop Shirley knows that Jesus is her source of enthusiasm and life. Her eternal fruit can only come from the eternal source. Your roots control your fruits.

Other Men and Women Showing P.R.I.D.E

Shirley's life is a great example of P.R.I.D.E's conceptual map. History has given us examples of many great leaders who have also lived P.R.I.D.Efully. Gandhi, Rosa Parks, Thomas Jefferson, Jesse Jackson, Abraham Lincoln, Henry Louis Gates, Alice Walker, Oprah Winfrey, and Michael Jackson, just to name a few. You can also find examples of individuals with P.R.I.D.E in people in your own life or strangers you meet along the way.

Here are some other's stories…

P-PURPOSE: Mahatma Ghandi

Ghandi was a man of purpose. Once, he said, "The main purpose of life is to live rightly, think rightly and act rightly. The soul must languish when we give all our thoughts to our body." His purpose was to be peace itself and spread peace throughout the world. Ghandi was a major political and spiritual leader in India and the Indian Independence movement. He was the pioneer of Satyagraha- a philosophy that is largely concerned with truth and resistance to evil through active, non-violent resistance'- which led India to independence and inspired movements for civil rights and freedom across the world. Ghandi was a source of inspiration and brought purpose in others like Martin Luther King, who modeled his movement.

R-RESPECT: Thomas Jefferson

Jefferson was one of the authors of the Declaration of Independence, and served as both a founding father and president for the United States. Jefferson was a committed Republican- arguing passionately for liberty, democracy, and devolved power. Jefferson also wrote the statute for religious freedom in 1777- which was adopted by the state of Virginia in 1786. This was one of the first bills on religious tolerance in the country. Thomas Jefferson fostered a belief in human rights and is known to have possessed. Because of this, he is known to have possessed the trait of respect, becoming one of the most respectable persons in history.

I-INTEGRITY: Maya Angelou

When you read the work of Maya Angelou or just glimmer it through her well-circulated and impactful quotes, you see her deep understanding of right and wrong. Maya had a talent of turning stories that engaged and challenged you as a reader without even realizing it. By the end of one of her stories, you will often find yourself questioning life and what you can do to assist and uplift others. She's a queen for integrity, may her soul rest in peace and continue to inspire moral living amongst us.

D-DETERMINATION: Thomas Edison

More than anyone in history, Thomas Edison is responsible for the modern world in which we live today. He was born in 1847 to working class parents. His curiosity drove him to test out the trials and errors of many prior innovations that would lead him to his own patent in 1093. When he was a young boy, his teacher told him that he was too stupid to learn anything. "I never quit until I get what I'm after." He replied. "Negative results are just what I'm after. They're just as valuable as positive results." It took him 2000 tries to correctly make the incandescent light bulb, but he was determined to succeed in the face of failure.

E-ENTHUSE: Michael Jackson

In the P.R.I.D.E model, enthuse means to possess the spirit of God, being full of life and energy. Michael Jackson encompassed this trait. Once called, "the King of Pop", he spent his music career making enthusiastic, upbeat pop tracks for all the world to hear. He started out as a young child as a member in the Jackson 5. From there, he used his power of enthusiasm to influence his listeners for the better, producing multiple #1 tracks on the pop charts.

Claude Brown

Import and Sports Car Specialist/Business Owner (90 Year Old Pioneer)

1928-Present

Claude Brown blazed a lifelong record of building and working on imports and sports cars while learning the business of setting up others in business located in Clemson and the upstate of South Carolina

Claude Brown was born in Sandy Springs of Anderson County in South Carolina to a sharecroppers' family. Brown's career as a mechanic started when he spent two years in the United States Army, serving in France and Germany. The Army learned that Claude had a passion for mechanical and automotive skills and assigned him to the motor pool working on cars for generals and privates. He took this opportunity to learn the French and German cultures, building sports cars and conducting business. Brown returned to South Carolina where he became the first black man to own a gas station (Philips 66) where he employed several employees, black and white. At this point, his services as an automotive specialist were in demand from Clemson University engineers, upstate South Carolina, and even those from as far away as Atlanta, Georgia.

Claude Brown is the only living auto-specialist who continues to practice his skills at his age. Many that he helped to set up in business have passed on. During the civil rights movement in the '60's, Mr. Brown bought school buses to transport black students to their schools as well as seniors to doctors' visits. He is most proud that he worked on Harvey Gantt's car, the first black student to attend Clemson University. Mr. Gantt graduated as an engineer and became the mayor of Charlotte, North Carolina.

Even today, Mr. Brown continues to work on imported automobiles and give business tips to others. His claim to fame and his turning point as a business man happened almost 50 years ago when he recognized that an establishment was using his mechanical skills and knowledge; paying him $25 a week as the business owners were profiting as much as $250. At this point, he opened his own business and insisted others do the same. He gave a toolbox to everyone he set up in business and he continues this practice even today. His toolbox gift deals with the concept that if they lose the shop or building to practice, they can still practice and make money for their family because they have a toolbox that can travel. Mr. Brown had the experience of losing his buildings at least three times in the past, but his motto is **you can take my building, but you can't take my toolbox**.

OPERATION PRIDE CONCEPTUAL MAP

Purpose	**Respect**	**Integrity**	**Discipline**	**Enthusiasm**
Proactive, Purpose, Prayer, Perseverance	Valuing Self and others	Truth and honesty	Consistently following through [responsibility. Do what you have to do (before or not after the deadline) when you are suppose to do it.	Joy in completion
				Great excitement and interest
				Spiritual involvement
				Thanksgiving
				Support and respect for leadership "Enthuse" the Spirit of God

Kwanzaa Community Values

The summary of Nguzo Saba Formed with the Acronym PRIDE

Out of Kwanzaa values P.R.I.D.E. values are derived: learning activities are the result

Kwanzaa values = P.R.I.D.E. values; these values lead to 12 Life Skills

NGUZO SABA (the Seven Principles)

Umoja = Unity - to strive for and maintain unity in the family, community, nation, and race

Kujicagulia = Self etermination to define ourselves and speak for ourselves, instead of being defined, named, created and spoken for by

PRIDE (5 Cultural Values)

P-Perseverance, purpose proactive. PRIDE

R-respect

I-Integrity

D-Discipline

12 Life Skills

1. Decision making with P.R.I.D.E.
2. Careers and Jobs with P.R.I.D.E.
3. Communicating with P.R.I.D.E.
4. Understanding the Value of Self Knowledge with P.R.I.D.E.
5. Accepting oneself with P.R.I.D.E.
6. Leadership with P.R.I.D.E.
7. Understanding the Value of the Knowledge of Spirituality with

P.R.I.D.E.

8. Working with Groups with P.R.I.D.E.

9. Managing with P.R.I.D.E.

10. Business Management with P.R.I.D.E.

11. Developing Relationships with P.R.I.D.E.

12. Transfer of knowledge with P.R.I.D.E.

E-Enthusiasm

others.

Ujima= Collective work and responsibility to build and maintain our community together and make our sisters and brothers problems our problems and solve them together.

Ujamaa- Cooperative economics.

Nia= Purpose to make our collective vocation the building and developing to our community in order to restore our people to their traditional greatness.

Kuumba = Creativity-to do always as much as we can, in the way we can, in order to leave our community more beautiful and beneficial than we inherited it

Imanu=Faith-to believe with all our hearts in our people, our teachers, our leaders and the righteousness and victory of our struggle.

The Psychology and Challenges of P.R.I.D.E. for Your Journey

I believe like Socrates:

- Evil and wrongdoing were based on ignorance

- That men fought wars because they didn't know any better

- That racial prejudice was based on the lack of knowledge

- That man exploited man because he needed to be enlightened

- That power corrupts, and absolute power corrupts absolutely

But, we know that knowledge is not enough and that man:

- Can know the truth and deliberately lie

- Can see the good and deliberately choose evil

- Can see the light and deliberately walk in darkness

- Can see the high road and deliberately choose the low road

I'm convinced, through the results of P.R.I.D.E research, that man does what he does because he does not possess: P-PURPOSE, R-RESPECT, I-INTERGRITY, D-DETERMINATION, and E-ENTHUSE (the Spirit of God). These are all the roots that control your fruits. This concept must be taught, internalized, and practiced if all men are to be maximized in the spirit. Only then can we coexist in harmony, like Shirley. "Truckstop Shirley" has earned her P.R.I.D.E. degree. She is in harmony with all mankind.

Dedication

Family

To my two sons, Keenan and Kyle, who both died at ages far too young. They both demonstrated such strong, natural skills in speaking, and debating civil and equal rights. They were and will always be loved and remembered for everything they were and could have been.

To my parents, Willie and Elnora James. To my grandparents Nathan and Maggie Whitfield, and Oscar and Lula Blacknell. To my wife, Elouise, my daughter Kirstyn; my aunts Eva, Jan, Mary Florine, and Larine.

To my lovely and beautiful sisters and brothers, Annete, Bettie, Maggie Cathy, Rico, and Carlton. Thank you for your many words of encouragement, belief, and love.

Saints in Heaven

To my neighbors, as a child in Bradenton, FL, I was greatly influenced by Ida and Nate Jenkins, Mrs. Louise Hunter, Mrs. Mabell Robinson, Mrs. Lizzie Lee-Thomas, Ms. Jessie B. Miller, Early and Louise Hines, Mr. Mrs. Paul Manning, Mr. and Mrs. Walker Stewart, Jimmy Cromartie, Mr. and Mrs. Lewis Brown; how happy and lucky, how happy and lucky we were to have you as neighbors. Your compliments and belief that I would finish college, get a Ph.d., and write many books and poetry has always sustained me. Although, you've passed on, I will never forget that God placed the greatness and talents in me but, it was through your kind words and smiles that they are ignited. I will forever pass this burning torch of enthusiasm to others regardless of their religion, color and social background.

*

The mighty oak was once a nut that held its ground. We're all a mighty oak in the making, and it's all right to be a little nutty as long as we hold our ground!

Special Thanks

To my research assistants: Kiana Gilchrist, Erica Kim, Ekei Eyo and Arielle James-Muhammad, Vince Cartee.

To my academic counselor, Dr. Eugene Herrington (Morehouse College).

To my legal mentors, Attorney James Hadnott, and Steve Chapman.

To my editors, Nilza Santana-Castillo, and my wife, Elouise James.

Pat
(Board Member) Shirley Robert
(President)

About the Author

REV. DR. ROMANDO JAMES PH.D.

PRESIDENT & FOUNDER
OPERATION COMMON SENSE WITH PRIDE MINISTRIES
CLEMSON UNIVERSITY, PROFESSOR EMERITIS

Office: (864) 650-2891
Fax: (864) 654-4070

P.O. Box 1713
Clemson, SC 29633

operationPRIDE@yahoo.com
prideclemson.wix.com/operationpride

Rev. Dr. Romando James', Ph.D. Introduction

Rev. Dr. Romando James, Professor Emeritus, Clemson University, received degrees in five different areas from four different schools: Ph.D. from Clark Atlanta University (Counseling and Psychology), M.A. from Clark Atlanta (Counseling), M.A from Jersey City State University (Reading), Ed.S. from Rutgers University (Supervision and Administration), and a B.S from Florida A&M University (Education and Drama). He then left the control system of education to pursue a movement known as **Operation Common Sense with P.R.I.D.E. Ministries.** Romando's movement derives from his life experiences and his doctorate dissertation: "The Perceived Effects of Social Alienation on African - American College Students Enrolled at a Predominantly White-American Southern University." His dissertation led to the design and development of the P.R.I.D.E . **(Purpose-Respect-Integrity-Determination-Enthusiasm)** Scale, the principal instrument used to test and evaluate social alienation experiences by African-Americans. The P.R.I.D.E. movement has brought about numerous opportunities for service and recognition. A member of the **Omega Psi Phi** fraternity, he was able to use P.R.I.D.E. Rites of Passage movement for training 2000 African-American males. James also received recognition from the South Carolina House of Representatives in 1998 and again in 2003; and he was awarded the **Jefferson Award,** the **Nobel Prize** for Public Service in South Carolina. In **March of 2010** Dr. James was awarded **Man of the Year from Mt. Sinai World Outreach Ministry.** He was also invited to preach in the countries of Nicaragua and Columbia. He is a national member of the board of Habitat for Humanity.

Dr. James received the **Distinguished Service Award** from the South Carolina State School of Business and the **Outstanding Alumni Service Award** in Education from Clark Atlanta University for his research in education. These awards recognized Dr. James' research concerning the **Effects of Social Alienation** of black college students. Additionally, Dr. James was honored and listed with the **Family Heritage House Bradenton, FL with other Outstanding Visionary Black Floridians**, which include but was not limited to **James Weldon Johnson, General Daniel (Chappie) James, Zora Hurston, A. Phillip Randolph and James (Buck) O'Neil.**

In February 2006, **Dr. James was invited to present his P.R.I.D.E. research in Baton. Rouge, LA at the 14th Annual International NAAAS Conference.**

His presentation was made before:

- The National Association of African American Studies,

- The National Association of Hispanic and Latino Studies,

- The National Association of Native American Studies,

- The International Association of Asian Studies, and

- The study of Islamic and Middle Eastern Studies

Dr. James was invited to present his P.R.I.D.E. research in Beijing, China during the 2008 Olympics.

Dr. James has held many positions in the field of education. He has served as a full professor in the Department of Family and Youth Development at Clemson University. He was selected as a presidential intern and later served as a **Senior Research Fellow for the Huston National Center**. Dr. James was an associate professor at Rutgers University as well as a public school teacher in Florida, New Jersey, and South Carolina. His claim to fame came as a teacher when he **advised, counseled, and taught the young people who formed a jazz band now known as "Kool and the Gang".**

Dr. James' life experiences have been the subject of a few documentaries, including "Jars Full of Ideas", "Living Your Choices, Romando", and "A Musical History of Agriculture in America." But this is not his only connection with film; **Dr. James is a consultant for HBO** for "The Dwight Miller Story", derived from his book **Lynch My Body, But Not my Soul**.

Dr. James also excels in his written work. His many publications include: "Double Standards of Justice, Its Genesis, Its Revelation" (1998), **"The Effects of Social Alienation on Black College Students on a White Campus (1995), "The Role of Boys Club and Juvenile Delinquency in Newark, NJ during the 60s and 70s riots"**, and **Integrated Expressive and Preforming Arts Manual** (1987). His poetry can be found internationally, and he is registered with the **Library of Congress**. Some of these publications include: **"When I Fly Man's Plane"** (1991), **"Mother Was Always Home"**(1999), **"Point Guard with P.R.I.D.E."** (1998), **"The American Flag-Red, White, and Blue -Why Do We Need Two"** (2000), **"Truck Stop Shirley"** (2007), **"Too Poor for the Projects, Too Rich For The White House"** (2008), **"Give Into David"** (2008), **"The Night the Car Wouldn't Start** (2008). **"Voices Crying in the Wilderness"** (2015).

His ministry has produced poets, writers, authors, preachers, bishops, Ph.D.s, professional authors, lawyers, and one very special **Miss Black USA 1987.**

Burbach, Harold J., and Myron A. Thompson, III."Note on Alienation, Race and College Attribution." Psychological Reports (June 12, 1973): 273-274.

Burbach, Harold J., and Myron A. Thompson, III .The Development of a Contextual Measure of Alienation. Charlotteville, VA: University of Virginia, 1972.

Burke, Joan M. Civil Rights: A Current Guide to the People, Organizations, and Events. New York: R. R. Bowker Co., 1974.

Burrell, Leon F., and Toni B. Trombley. "Academic Advising Minority Students on Predominantly White Campuses." Journal of College student Personnel (March 1983): 117-121.

Butler, Reginald. "Implications of Black-Consciousness Process Model." Psychotherapy Theory, Research, and Practice 12, no. 4 (Winter 1975): 407-411.

Clark, John P.   "Measuring Alienation with a Social System." American Social Review 26 (December 1969): 849-852.

Clark, Reginald."Why Poor, Black Children Succeed or Fail." Family Life and School Achievement (June 1981): 61-64.

Clark, Reginald."Profile of the Low Achievers."Family Life and School Achievement (June 1981): 183-185.

Coachman, W. "Guest in a Strange House." Paper presented at a meeting of the Illinois Committee of African American Concerns in Higher Education, University Park, Illinois, 1985.

Coleman, J. c., and W. E. Broen. Abnormal Psychology and Modern Life, 4th ed. Glenview, IL: Scott Foresman, 1972.

Coleman, J. S., and J. McPartland. Eguality of Educational Opportunity. Glenview, IL: Scott Foresman, 1966.

Dean, D. G., and R. Middleton. "Alienation: Its Meaning and Measurement." American Sociological Review (1961): 753-758.

Epps, B."Black Campus Life. "Journal of College Students (July 1978): 78-79.

Epps, E. G. "Negro Academic Motivation and Performance: An overview." Journal of social Issues (June 1969): 5-11.

Fleming, Jacqueline. African Americans in College. San Francisco: Jossey-Bass, 1984.

Fleming, Jacqueline. "African American Women in White College Environments."Journal of Social Issues 39 (March 1983): 41-54.

Fleming, Jacqueline. "Black Women in Black and White College Environments: The Making of a Matriarch." Journal of Social Issues (January 1984): 41-53.

Fleming, Jacqueline."Black Women in Black and White College Environments." Journal of Social Issues (June 1990): 56-58.

Fleming, R., G. Nelson, Pruitt Gibbs, and F. Harper. "Racism on Predominantly White College Campuses." Journal of College Students (June 1969): 23.

Franklin, A. J. "What Clinicians Should Know About Testing Black Students." Negro Educational Review 28 (1977): 202-218.

Freedle, R., and I. Kostin."Item Difficulty of Four Verbal Item Types and an Index of Differential Item Functioning for Black and White Examinees." Journal of Educational Measurement 27 (1990): 329-343.

Gaines-Carter, P. "Is My "Post-Integration" Daughter African American Enough?"Ebony, September 1985, 54- 56.

Galicki, s., and M. McEwen. "Black Americans on White Campuses." Journal of College Student Development (September 1989): 389.

Gordon, Edmund. "Protection of Ethnicity." Review Committee (1991): 98.

Gordon, Edmund and Francis Roberts. "One Nation, Many People: A Declaration of Cultural Interdependence."The Report of the NYS Social Studies Review Development Committee (June 1991): 41-46.

Graham, Calvin, et al."Prior Interactial Experience." Journal of Personality (May 1985): 1146-1154.

Green, R. V. "An Institution-Wide Standardized Test-Taking Skills Development Program."Paper presented at the 7th Annual Conference on the Preparation and survival of African American Public School Teachers, Norfolk, VA, 1986.

Herrington, Eugene. "The Experience of the African American Male Adolescent in Psychotherapy." Ph.D. diss., California Institute of Integral Studies, San Francisco, California, 1989.

Isaac, Stephen, and William B. Michael. Handbook in Research and Evaluation. California: Edits Publishing Co., 1981.

Jackson, James D. "Alienation and Interactional styles in a Predominantly White University." Journal of College Students (February 1983): 54-57.

James, Romando. PRIDE Scale. Clemson, SC: Operation Common Sense, 1992.

Johnson, Debra King, Ph.D. Longitudinal Studies of Black Students at Clemson University. Clemson, SC: Clemson University, 1992.

Johnson, S. T., and M. B. Wallace. "Characteristics of SAT Quantitative Items Showing Improving After Coaching Among Black Students From Low-Income Families: An Exploratory study." Journal of Educational Measurement 26 (1989): 133-145.

Jones, Reginald. Black Psychology. Newberry Park, CA: Harper and Row Publishers, 1980.

Jones, Reginald L. "An Abridged Version of the 1975 Commission on Standardized Testing Report to APGA." In African American Psychology, ed. Reginald L. Jones, 177-185. New York: Harper & Row, 1980.

Kazalunas, J. R. "The Testing of African American Students." Clearinghouse 52 (1979): 195-198.

Larke, James P., and McConnell E. McJamerson. "Minorities in Higher Education." Paper presented at the Annual Meeting of American Educational Research Association, San Francisco, CA, March 27-31, 1989.

Lesser, G. "Mental Abilities of Children from Different Social Classes." Monographs of the Society (1965): 7.

Maxwell, Grace R. "The civil Rights Movement and African American Participants." As cited in The Civil Rights Movement in Florida and the United states, ed. Charles V. Smith, 252-253. Tallahassee, Florida: Father and Son Publishing, Inc., 1969.

Maulana, Karengra. Kwanzaa: A Celebration of Family, Community and Culture, 2nd Edition, Los Angeles: University of Sankore Press, 2008

McClung, Jacquetta, Gerald L. Waddle and Carmen Harris. A Study to Identify Factors that Contribute to African American Student Withdrawal at Clemson University. A Report of Report completed under the Institution Grants Program for Student Retention Activities. Clemson, SC: South Carolina Commission on Higher Education, 1988.

McCullock, Jock."Black Soul, White Artifact." In Fanon's Clinical Psychology and Social Theory, 118-135. New York, NY: Cambridge University Press, 1983.

Meredith, James. Three Years in Mississippi. Bloomington, London: Indiana University Press, 1966.

Middleton, Russell."Alienation, Race and Education." Pacific Review (December 1973): 973-977.

Miller, L. P."Testing Black Students:Implications for Assessing Inner-City Schools."Journal of Negro Education 44 (1975): 406-420.

Myers, Linda, and Kendal Hini. Understanding an Afrocentric Workman.Ohio: World View Publishing, 1990.

New York State Education Department Study. of Racial and Social Class Isolation in tte Schools. New York: Office of Research and Evaluation, New York State Education Department, 1969.

Noble, Wade."Psychological Nigrescence."The Counseling Psychologist 17, no. 2 (April 1989): 7-8.

Nyquist, Ewald B.Racial and Soclal Class Isolation. New York, NY: New York State Department, 1968.

Pope, Davis. "The Influence of White Racial Identity Attitudes."Journal of Psychology (1986): 388-394.

Pounds, Augustine w. "Black Students Needs on Predominantly White Campuses."In Responding to the Needs of Today's Minority students, ed. D. Wright, 29-33. San Francisco: Jessey-Bass, 1987.

Quevedo, Garcia, ed."From the Field."Journal of Student Development (January 1989): 32-33.

Schmitt, A. P., and N. J. Dorans."Differential Item Functioning for Minority Examinees on the SAT." Journal of Educational Measurement 27 (1990): 67-81.

Sedlacek, W. E."Black Students on White Campuses." Journal of College Personnel (May 1987): 84-95.

Seeman, N. 11 0n the Meaning of Alienation. 11 American Sociological Review (1959): 783-791.

Siggelkiov, A. "Racism in Higher Education: A Permanent Condition? "Journal of College Student Development 81 (January 1991): 125-127.

Southern Regional Education Board. The Black Student on Campus: A Project Report. Atlanta, GA: Southern Regional Education Board, 1971.

Sowell, Thomas. Black Education: Myths and Tragedies. New York: Davis McKay Co., Inc., 1970.

Steward, Robbie J., Marshall R. Jackson, and James D. Jackson. 11 Alienation and Interactional Styles in a Predominantly White Environment: A Study of Successful Black Students. 11 Journal of College Student Development 31 (November 1990): 509-515.

Suen, Hoi K.11 Alienation and Attrition of Black College Students on a Predominantly White Campus."Journal of College Student Personnel (Mnrch 1983): 117-121.

Taub Debra, and Marylu McEwen. " The Relationship of Racial Identity Attitudes. " Journal of Psychology (March 1980): 15.

Taylor, Charles A. "A Report of Isolation." Journal of College Student Personnel 12 (February 1986): 30.

Thomas, Rose, and John Greenya. Black Leaders: Then and Now. Garrett Park, MD: Garrett Park Press, 1984.

Torrance, James. "Creative Positive Strategy." Journal of College Student Development (March 1976): 18.

Trillin, Calvin. An Education in Georgia. Athens and London: The University of Georgia Press, 1964.

Trippi, Joseph and Stanley Baker. " Cultural Differences in African American College Students." Journal of College Student Development 30 (March 1989): 7-8.

University of New York. Racial and Social Class Isolation in Schools. A Report to the Board of Regents. New York: University of New York, 1969.

U.S. Commission on civil Rights. Racial Isolation in the Public Schools. New York, NY: New York State Education Department, 1967.

Printed in the United States
By Bookmasters